Comfort Food
for
Sharing,
Caring & Giving

Food to make for others.

by
Norma Bannerman, PHEc and Laurana Rayne, PHEc
with the help of many

Cover illustration by: Richard Adie
Other illustrations by: Brandie Cormier

Canadian Cataloguing in Publication Data
Bannerman, Norma.
  Comfort food for sharing, caring and giving

(Comfort foods series)
Includes index.
ISBN 0-9683165-5-7

ISBN 0-9683165-0-6 (for the complete set of six books)

1. Cookery. I. Rayne, Laurana, 1946- II. Title. III. Series.
TX714.B364 1998   641.5   C97-911095-5

Titles in this set:

red	**Comfort Food for Cold Days** *Food that warms the body and soul.*
orange	**Comfort Food for Families** *Food that nourishes and nurtures.*
yellow	**Comfort Food for Company** *Meals to share with friends.*
green	**Comfort Food with a Heritage** *Food that connects us with our roots.*
blue	**Comfort Food for Sharing, Caring and Giving** *Food to make for others.*
violet	**Comfort Food for Congenial Times** *Recipes for relaxed visiting.*

Published by:

Hummingbird Wings
Box 63066
2604 Kensington Road NW
Calgary, Alberta, Canada
T2N 4S5

phone   (403) 270-3052
fax   (403) 270-1883
internet http://www.cadvision.com/nollind/cfcb/

Books are available from the publisher through the above address. Send a cheque or money order (in Canadian funds) payable to Hummingbird Wings in the amount of $5.95 per book plus shipping and handling (as follows) and applicable taxes (GST and PST).

Number of books	Shipping and handling
1	$ 2.00
2 - 3	$ 2.50
4 - 18	$ 6.00

Note: orders for complete sets of the six titles include an attractive slip case.

Note: shipping rates are for within Canada only and are subject to change

Mastercard or VISA orders can be placed by telephoning the publisher or through the web site.

Designed, printed and produced in Canada

From the authors...

About these books...

Our call to the public for comfort food recipes included a request for a few sentences as to why the contributors found their recipes to be comfort foods.

Over 300 recipes were received, and as we read the contributors' heart warming "stories", we began to see that comfort foods are more than good food — they also carry a loving message, and like love, they have many facets. They can be hot soup on a cold day, great grandmother's biscuits warm from the oven, rice pudding for someone ill, a hearty casserole for someone bereaved, a pot of stew for a new mother, or a thoughtfully chosen meal for friends. In the preparing, serving and sharing, comfort foods connect us with others in a meaningful way; they become part of the "glue" that holds us together.

From the recipes and stories received these six books were born, each with its own unique theme. Each contributor's reason for choosing a recipe precedes it. Additional comments and anecdotal material appear at the foot of many of the pages.

We hope the Comfort Food Books are something more than good additions to your recipe collection — it is our wish that they become a means of conveying loving messages to your families and friends.

About these recipes...

Recipes were submitted in many forms, formatted and typed by volunteer home economists, then triple tested. Recipes calling for ground beef were tested with ground chicken; those calling for sour cream were tested with yogurt; recipes using mayonnaise were tested with light mayonnaise. The substitutes worked well and are given as alternatives.

Recipes were written in both Imperial and Metric measures. Most Metric measures are the equivalents recommended by the Metric Commission:

$$2 \text{ tbsp} - 25 \text{ ml}$$
$$3 \text{ tbsp} - 50 \text{ mL}$$
$$4 \text{ tbsp } (\text{1/4 cup}) - 50 \text{ mL}$$

Sometimes, though, we achieved better results when an amount closer to the Imperial measure was used:

$$2 \text{ tbsp} - 30 \text{ mL}$$
$$3 \text{ tbsp} - 45 \text{ mL}$$
$$4 \text{ tbsp } (\text{1/4 cup}) - 60 \text{ mL}$$

Where recipes call for one or more cups of flour, the Metric equivalent of 250 mL (more than 1 cup) can produce dry products. We experienced this with some recipes where the flour/liquid ratio is critical, for example, the Cream Biscuits in *Comfort Food for Company*. In such cases, the Metric flour amounts were reduced.

It was a great pleasure to receive, sort and read the recipes and their stories, then to taste the wonderful products that resulted. We hope your experience is equally pleasurable!

The funds generated by these books will be dedicated to:

- improving the health and quality of life of children and their families, and
- initiating ventures that contribute to quality of life

Comfort Food for
Sharing, Caring and Giving
Food to make for others.

**Comfort food is nurturing,
wholesome and soul-satisfying.
It cheers the hearts of others.**

Foods to Share — pages 8 - 24

Food taken to potlucks and
to friends experiencing busy
or stressful times brings them
pleasure and comfort.

Foods that Say I Care — pages 25 - 36

Food prepared with love
nurtures and heals those
who are ill or convalescing.

Gifts of Food — pages 37 - 42

Food thoughtfully made for
others warms the hearts of
both the giver and the receiver.

More recipes to make for others found in other books in this set...

Suitable for potlucks or to take to friends...

Comfort Food for Families

Three-Cheese Lasagna
Good Ol' Beans and Rice
Cheese and Onion Quick Bread
Mrs. Kelly's Chocolate Cake
Queen Elizabeth Cake

Comfort Food for Congenial Times

Easy Chicken Cannelloni
Artichoke and Spinach Casserole
Noodle Lasagna
Greek Chick Pea Salad
Cranberry Streusel Coffee Cake

Comfort Food With a Heritage

Shepherd's Pie
French-Canadian Tourtière
Ice Box Ginger Cookies
Butter Tarts

Comfort Food for Company

Pineapple Carrot Cake
Banana Bundt Cake

Comfort Food for Cold Days

Dill Loaf
Whole Wheat Quick Bread

For ill and convalescing folks...

Comfort Food for Cold Days

Harvest Soup
Hearty Beef Soup
Oven-Baked Rice Pudding

Comfort Food for Families

Pat's Pea Soup
Celery Leaf Soup
Cream of Chicken Soup
Welsh Rarebit

Food gifts to give people...

Comfort Food with a Heritage

Sour Cream Scones
Very Datey Date Loaf
Ice Box Ginger Cookies
Butter Tarts

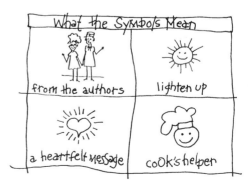

What the Symbols Mean

from the authors | lighten up
a heartfelt message | cook's helper

Recipes to make for others.

Comfort food cheers the hearts of others.

Comfort Casserole

"This is what I always take to friends who are ill or when there is a funeral. It's also a delicious company casserole."

¹/₄ cup	butter, margarine or vegetable oil	50 mL
2 tsp.	finely chopped green pepper	10 mL
2 tsp.	finely chopped onion	10 mL
¹/₂ cup	sliced fresh or canned mushrooms	125 mL
¹/₄ cup	all-purpose flour	50 mL
2 cups	chicken broth	500 mL
¹/₂ cup	grated Cheddar cheese	125 mL
2 cups	cubed cooked chicken or turkey	500 mL
2 cups	crushed potato chips	500 mL

Preheat oven to 350°F (180°C). Have ready an ungreased 6-cup (1.5 L) casserole.

Melt butter in a large frying pan or saucepan over medium heat. Cook green pepper, onion and mushrooms for about 3 minutes or until onion has softened. Stir in flour. Add broth and cook, stirring frequently, until mixture boils and thickens. Remove from heat.

Add cheese, stirring until cheese is melted and sauce is smooth. Gently mix in chicken.

Spread 1 cup (250 mL) potato chips in bottom of casserole. Carefully spoon chicken mixture evenly over top. Cover with remaining potato chips. Bake for about 25 minutes or until bubbly and heated through. Remove from oven and let stand 10 minutes before serving.
Makes about 4 servings.

May be prepared in advance and refrigerated until baking time. Allow 5 - 10 minutes longer for baking.

Foods to Share

Food taken to potlucks and to friends experiencing busy or stressful times brings them pleasure and comfort.

*Comfort Food for **Sharing**, Caring, and Giving*

Oriental Chicken or Turkey

"Every time I cook a turkey, we save enough meat to make this recipe. It's easy, colourful and tastes so good."

3 cups	cubed cooked chicken or turkey	750 mL
2 cups	sliced celery	500 mL
1 cup	chopped onion	250 mL
1 cup	diced green or red pepper, or mixture of both	250 mL
2	cans (4 oz/113 g each) chow mein noodles	2
2	cans (10 fl oz/284 mL each) cream of mushroom soup	2
1	can (10 fl oz/284 mL) water	1
2 tbsp.	soy sauce	25 mL

Preheat oven to 325°F (160°C). Have ready an ungreased 12-cup (3 L) casserole or 9 x 13-inch (22 x 34 cm) baking dish.

In a large bowl, combine chicken or turkey, celery, onion, green pepper and noodles.

In a medium bowl, combine mushroom soup, water and soy sauce. Add to meat and vegetables; stir to combine. Spread in casserole or baking dish. Cover. Bake for 1 to 1 ¹/₂ hours or until piping hot.
Makes 8 - 10 servings.

Cooked poultry ready-to-go

Having cooked poultry on hand in your freezer broadens the scope of recipes you can put together quickly, so consider the following options:

Some grocery outlets now carry cut-up cooked chicken. If stores in your area don't carry this product, suggest they look into it.

When cooking a turkey, choose one larger than you need, then cut up and freeze leftovers in 2 or 3-cup quantities.

Roast a large chicken, enjoy your meal, then cut up and freeze leftovers in desired quantities.

Note: For a good way to use that turkey carcass, see Don's Turkey Soup on page 12 of the Comfort Food for Cold Days book.

Comfort food cheers the hearts of others.

No-Boil Lasagna

"When friends are going through a stressful time due to illness, grieving, or the birth of a new baby, I always take them a pan of this lasagna. It tastes great and is very nutritious as it includes all the food groups!"

1 lb.	ground beef	500 g
1	medium onion, chopped	1
1/4 tsp.	garlic powder	1 mL
2	cans (14 fl oz/398 mL each) tomato sauce	2
1	can (10 fl oz/284 mL) sliced mushrooms, undrained	1
1/2 cup	water	125 mL
1 tsp.	dried oregano	5 mL
1	egg	1
1 cup	creamed cottage cheese	250 mL
1/4 cup	grated Parmesan cheese	50 mL
1 tsp.	salt	5 mL
1	package (300 g) frozen spinach, thawed, chopped and thoroughly drained (optional)	1
15	regular lasagna noodles, uncooked	15
1	package (170 g) sliced mozzarella cheese	1

Have ready an ungreased 9 x 13-inch (22 x 34 cm) baking pan.

In a large saucepan over medium heat, brown beef and onion; drain off fat. Add garlic powder. Stir in tomato sauce, mushrooms and their liquid, water and oregano. Bring to a boil, then remove from the heat.

In a large bowl, beat egg. Mix in cottage cheese, Parmesan cheese and salt. Stir in chopped spinach.

Spoon a third of the meat sauce into the bottom of the baking pan. Cover with five noodles; repeat. Spread cheese and spinach mixture over noodles. Cover with remaining noodles and sauce. Top with cheese slices. Cover with foil, and place pan on baking sheet.

Set oven at 375°F (190°C) and bake for 45 minutes. Uncover and continue baking for about 15 minutes or until brown.
Makes about 9 servings.

Comfort Food for **Sharing**, Caring, and Giving

Tummy-Warming Noodle Bake

"Recently, I prepared six times the quantity of this recipe to take to a pot luck dinner, and I didn't bring <u>any</u> home!"

2 ¹/₂ cups	uncooked noodles or macaroni	625 mL
1 lb.	ground beef, chicken or turkey	500 g
1	small onion, chopped	1
¹/₂ tsp.	garlic powder (or 1 clove, crushed)	2 mL
1	can (10 fl oz/284 mL) tomato soup	1
1	can (10 fl oz/284 mL) creamed corn	1
¹/₄ cup	ketchup	60 mL
1 cup	grated Cheddar cheese	250 mL

Preheat oven to 350°F (180°C). Have ready an ungreased 10-cup (2.5 L) casserole.

In a large pot, cook noodles in boiling water, with 1 tbsp. (15 mL) salt added, until just tender.

Meanwhile, in a large frying pan over medium heat, cook ground meat and onion until meat is no longer pink and onion is softened. Drain off fat. Stir in garlic, tomato soup, corn and ketchup; then gently mix in cooked noodles.

Turn into casserole and top with grated cheese; cover. Bake for about 45 minutes. Uncover and continue baking for about 10 minutes or until golden. *Makes 4 - 6 servings.*

Serve with a green vegetable or salad.

This may be made ahead and frozen before baking. Bake directly from the frozen state, allowing about 1 ¹/₂ hours covered and 10 minutes uncovered.

Freezing an unbaked casserole...

To free up your casserole dish, and to take less space in the freezer, line the dish with freezer wrap and spoon in casserole mixture. Cover and freeze. When it is completely frozen, lift from the dish and wrap well with additional freezer wrap. Label and put back in freezer.

When ready to use, remove freezer wrap and place casserole back in the original dish; it will fit nicely. Reheat as directed in the recipe. If there are no directions, assume that the frozen casserole will take at least one and one-half times as long as the casserole's regular baking time.

Comfort food cheers the hearts of others.

Cabbage Rolls

"These meaty cabbage rolls are a real favourite at home or for potlucks and large gatherings."

1	large head green cabbage	1
2 tbsp.	vegetable oil	25 mL
1 ½ cups	chopped onion, divided	375 mL
2 tsp.	salt	10 mL
2 tsp.	paprika	10 mL
½ tsp.	pepper	2 mL
½ cup	hot water	125 mL
3 lb.	ground beef	1.5 kg
1 ½ cups	uncooked long grain rice	375 mL
2 tsp.	salt	10 mL
½ tsp.	pepper	2 mL
1	can (28 fl oz/796 mL) tomato sauce	1
1	can (14 fl oz/398 mL) tomato juice	1
¼ cup	brown sugar	50 mL
1 tbsp.	lemon juice	15 mL

Wash and core cabbage, removing any damaged outer leaves. Place up-side-down in a large deep pot. Pour boiling water into the area where core was removed; continue until cabbage is covered with water. Cover and simmer for about 20 minutes, turning cabbage as needed. As outer leaves become soft enough to roll, remove them with tongs. Shave off the thick rib of each leaf to make rolling easier.

Heat vegetable oil in a roasting pan large enough to hold rolls. Add 1 cup (250 mL) of the chopped onion and cook for about 5 minutes, stirring occasionally, until softened. Sprinkle with salt, paprika and pepper. Pour in hot water. Remove from heat.

In a large bowl, combine uncooked ground beef, rice, the remaining chopped onion, salt and pepper. Put a large spoonful of this mixture on each leaf. Roll up leaf loosely, leaving a bit of room for filling to expand. Tuck in ends to make a neat compact bundle, and arrange rolls in layers on the bed of onions in the roasting pan. (See next page for tip about dealing with damaged leaves.)

In a medium bowl, combine tomato sauce, tomato juice, brown sugar and lemon juice. Pour over rolls; cover. Set oven at 325°F (160°C). Bake 2 to 2 ½ hours, until rice is tender. Add a bit of water during baking if necessary.

Makes about 3 dozen rolls, although number will vary depending on size of cabbage leaves.

*Comfort Food for **Sharing**, Caring, and Giving*

Corn Casserole

"To me, this is a typical comfort food — soft, warm and yummy."

3	large eggs (or 4 medium)	3
1 ¹/₃ cups	milk	325 mL
1 tsp.	salt	5 mL
¹/₄ tsp.	pepper	1 mL
5 tbsp.	all-purpose flour	75 mL
2	cans (14 fl oz/398 mL each) creamed corn	2
1	can (12 fl oz/341 mL) whole kernel corn, drained*	1

Preheat oven to 325°F (160°C). Grease an 8-cup (2 L) casserole dish.

In a large bowl, beat eggs, milk**, salt and pepper with an electric mixer. Beat in flour until smooth. Stir in creamed corn and kernel corn. Pour into casserole. Bake for 1 to 1 ¹/₂ hours or until set; the deeper the dish, the longer the baking time.

Makes 6 - 8 accompaniment servings; about 4 main-dish servings.

Sausage Corn Casserole: After mixing in corn, add 1 lb. (500 g) cooked sausage, cut in thirds, and a chopped green pepper which has been partially precooked.*** Pour into greased 12-cup (3 L) casserole. Bake as directed. Makes about 4 main-dish servings.

*   Or 1 1/2 cups (375 mL) cooked frozen corn.
**   If mixing by hand, whisk milk, flour, salt and pepper until smooth; whisk in eggs. Stir in creamed corn and kernel corn.
*** To precook the pepper, remove seeds, then dice the pepper. Microwave or cook briefly in a small amount of water until it has lost its crunchiness.

Patching cabbage leaves when making cabbage rolls...

When removing the softened leaves from the head of cabbage, some may be slightly damaged even if one is working as carefully as possible. If a leaf with a hole is used, some of the filling may come through, and it certainly isn't as attractive as a neat and tidy bundle.

There is no need to waste leaves with minor damage; simply patch them! To do this, place a small extra piece of cabbage inside the leaf, over the hole, before spooning on the filling. It holds everything in place, and is usually unnoticeable.

Texas Rice and Beans

"This recipe is an easy, excellent accompaniment for roast beef or barbecued steaks. It's good for potlucks, and can stand on its own as a main dish. The picante sauce gives this dish its final 'hotness', so choose the sauce according to your taste."

1	can (19 fl oz/540 mL) baked beans (or 2 ½ cups/625 mL)	1
1	can (14 fl oz/298 mL) tomatoes	1
1 cup	mild, medium or hot picante sauce	250 mL
½ cup	beer or apple juice	125 mL
¼ cup	brown sugar	50 mL
2 cups	cooked rice*	500 mL
¼ tsp.	salt	1 mL
¼ cup	slivered red onions (optional)	50 mL

In a large pot, combine beans, tomatoes, picante sauce, beer or apple juice, and brown sugar. Bring to a boil over high heat, then reduce heat and simmer uncovered for about 20 minutes to cook off some of the liquid and blend flavours; stir once or twice. Mix in rice and salt. Continue to cook, gently stirring once or twice, over low heat for about 10 minutes or until heated through. Garnish with red onions, if desired.

Makes 6 - 8 accompaniment servings; about 4 main-dish servings.

* Use leftover rice, or cook rice while beans are simmering. Check package for amounts of rice and water to give 2 cups (500 mL) cooked. Usually rice triples in volume, so you will need to start with about ⅔ cup (150 mL) uncooked rice and 1 ⅓ - 1 ½ cups (325 - 375 mL) water.

Comfort Food for **Sharing**, Caring, and Giving

Slurp!

"This recipe has become one of my favourites to take to potlucks or to friends going through troubled times. It has the most tantalizing aroma of anything I make, and it seems to intensify while being transported in a closed car to its destination."

1 lb.	ground beef, chicken or turkey	500 g
half	pouch dried onion soup mix	half
2	cans (14 fl oz/398 mL each) spaghetti with tomato sauce and cheese	2
1	can (14 fl oz/398 mL) tomato sauce	1
4	processed cheese slices, cut in half diagonally	4

Preheat oven to 350°F (180°C). Have ready an ungreased 8-cup (2 L) casserole dish.

Cook meat in a large frying pan over medium-high heat, stirring several times, until no pink colour remains. Drain off fat. Stir in onion soup mix. Add spaghetti and the tomato sauce; stir until just mixed. Transfer to casserole dish. Arrange cheese slices on top. Bake for about 45 minutes or until bubbly and heated through.
Makes 6 - 8 servings.

Soup that's rarely the same.

"It's been a long time since I made soup from a recipe. I did in the early years, and I still look at soup recipes for ideas. But most often, the soup I end up with depends on what needs to be used up from my fridge.

"I have two standard soup bases. One is a thin cream sauce. The other is chicken broth which I make from the bones when I cut up a chicken; I store the broth in the freezer until I need it.

"Sometimes I cook extra of a vegetable so I have leftovers for soup — mashed squash in a cream sauce with a touch of nutmeg is one of my favourites. Chicken broth with carrots, peas and noodles is particularly good with a bit of sliced green onion added during the last few minutes of cooking. But if I don't have carrots and peas, it might be celery and onion. And if I don't have squash, it could be canned tomatoes in the cream sauce."

Comfort food cheers the hearts of others.

Golden Rice

"This rice dish is attractive and delicious – I often take it to potlucks."

2 tbsp.	butter, margarine or vegetable oil	25 mL
1/2 cup	sliced celery	125 mL
1/2 cup	finely grated carrot	125 mL
	water	
1 cup	long grain brown rice	250 mL
1/2 cup	golden raisins*	125 mL
1	can (8 fl oz/227 mL) sliced water chestnuts, drained	1
2 tsp.	chicken bouillon base	10 mL
1/4 tsp.	salt	1 mL
1/4 cup	chopped roasted cashews	50 mL
1 tbsp.	dried parsley	15 mL

In a large saucepan with a tight-fitting lid, melt butter over medium-low heat. Add celery and carrot; cook uncovered, stirring occasionally, for about 5 minutes or until softened.

Meanwhile, check rice package to determine how much water is required to cook 1 cup (250 mL) of your brand of rice. Measure out that amount of water.

When vegetables are soft, add water, rice, raisins, water chestnuts, bouillon base and salt; stir. Bring to a boil over high heat. Cover, reduce heat, and cook for the length of time directed on the rice package, or until rice is soft and all liquid has been absorbed. If water has been absorbed before rice is fully tender, add a bit more hot water and continue cooking. When rice is cooked, stir in cashews and parsley.
Makes 4 - 6 servings.

*   Any raisins may be used, but golden are the most attractive in this dish.

I wonder?

Recently, I complimented my daughter-in-law on a delicious chicken dish she'd prepared. She smiled and said "You should like it, it's your recipe!" We had a good chuckle, then I began to wonder why other people's cooking always tastes better to me than my own. Perhaps it's those intangible ingredients they put into it.

Comfort Food for **Sharing**, Caring, and Giving

Barley Casserole

"This recipe was always brought to our annual summer potluck dinner by a dear fellow-instructor, and was always enjoyed by all."

2 tbsp.	butter, margarine or vegetable oil	25 mL
1 cup	chopped onion	250 mL
1 cup	diced celery	250 mL
1 cup	chopped fresh mushrooms*	250 mL
1/2 cup	chopped chives or green onion	125 mL
1 cup	pot barley, rinsed	250 mL
3	cans (10 fl oz/284 mL each) beef consomme**	3
1/4 cup	water**	50 mL
1/2 tsp.	pepper	2 mL
1/4 tsp.	salt	1 mL
1 cup	cashews (optional)	250 mL

Have ready an ungreased 8-cup (2 L) casserole.

Melt butter in a heavy frying pan over medium heat. Add onion and cook for about 5 minutes or until softened. Add celery, mushrooms, chives and barley. Cook, stirring frequently, for about 15 minutes, or until barley is lightly browned and celery is tender. Turn into casserole. Stir in consomme, water, salt and pepper. Cover.

Set oven at 350°F (180°C) and bake for about 1 1/2 hours. Sprinkle cashews over top and continue baking, covered, for another 30 minutes.
Makes 6 - 8 servings.

This is a wonderful addition to a steak, roast beef, pork or salmon dinner. It is also a very nice main dish on its own.

Clay Baker Method: Soak clay baker in water for 20 minutes. Prepare recipe as directed. Turn mixture into clay baker; cover. Place baker in cold oven. Set oven at 450°F (230°C). Bake for 30 minutes or until liquid is absorbed and barley is tender. Add cashews and bake 15 minutes longer.

*   If using canned mushrooms, use a 10 fl oz. (284 mL) can and drain well.
**   Instead of the consomme and water, 4 cups (1 L) water and 2 tbsp. (25 mL) beef bouillon base or 6 bouillon cubes may be used. It has a milder and slightly different flavour, but is also very good.

Isn't it comforting to know that...

A spillover in the oven won't smoke and burn (and is easier to clean up) if you sprinkle it liberally with salt as soon as it happens.

Comfort food cheers the hearts of others.

Calico Coleslaw

"I doubled this for a potluck last week. There wasn't a smidgen left."

8 cups	shredded cabbage*	2	L
1 cup	sliced green onions	250	mL
1 cup	diced Cheddar cheese	250	mL
¹/₂ cup	sliced ripe olives	125	mL
2	cans (12 fl oz/341 mL each) whole kernel, plain or Mexicorn, drained	2	
8	Roma tomatoes, diced	8	
1 cup	light or regular mayonnaise	250	mL
2 tbsp.	granulated sugar	30	mL
2 tbsp.	vinegar	30	mL
1 tsp.	celery seed	5	mL
1 tbsp.	prepared mustard	15	mL

In a very large bowl, combine cabbage, green onion, cheese, olives, corn and tomatoes.

In a small bowl, prepare dressing by thoroughly combining mayonnaise, sugar, vinegar, celery seed and prepared mustard. Add to cabbage mixture and toss to coat evenly. Cover and refrigerate for at least an hour to blend flavours.

Makes 12 - 16 servings.

*   Or use purchased cole slaw mixture available in supermarkets.

Calico Coleslaw

Peas and Cheese Pasta Salad

"This recipe came about because it contains all the favourite foods of my two-year old daughter. I've found that it pleases kids of all ages so I often take it to picnics and potlucks."

2 cups	uncooked pasta shells or spirals*	500	mL
2 cups	frozen green peas	500	mL
1/2 cup	diced Cheddar or marble cheese	125	mL
	dressing (either of recipes below)		

Cook the pasta in a large pot of boiling water with 1 tbsp. (15 mL) salt until almost tender; add peas and cook briefly until pasta is cooked and peas are tender-crisp. Drain. Rinse in cold water, and drain thoroughly. Mix in cheese.

Just before serving, pour one of the following dressings over salad and toss to mix.
Makes about 4 servings.

Cucumber Dressing

1/2 cup	regular or light mayonnaise	125	mL
2 tsp.	milk	10	mL
2 tbsp.	creamy cucumber dressing	25	mL

In a small bowl, combine all ingredients.

Tangy Dressing

1/2 cup	regular or light mayonnaise	125	mL
2 tbsp.	vinegar	30	mL
1 tbsp.	granulated sugar	15	mL
1/2 tsp.	prepared mustard	2	mL
1/4 tsp.	celery salt	1	mL

In a small bowl, combine all ingredients.

*   If substituting elbow macaroni, use only 1 1/3 cups (325 mL).

*Comfort Food for **Sharing**, Caring, and Giving*

Sea Foam Salad

"When my children planned a birthday supper, this salad was their first request. I have frequently served it for Christmas dinner and taken it to potluck dinners where it has been enjoyed."

2	cans (14 fl oz/396 mL each) pears packed in light syrup	2
1	package (85 g) lime jelly powder	1
1	package (8 oz/250 g) regular or light cream cheese, softened	1
2 tbsp.	regular or light mayonnaise or salad dressing	25 mL
½ cup	whipping cream, whipped (or 1 cup/250 mL whipped topping)	125 mL

Have ready a 6-cup (1.5 L) jelly mould. If you don't have a mould, the salad can be made in a bowl and served right from the bowl.

Drain pears, reserving syrup. Put pears into a small bowl, and mash them.

Into a small saucepan, measure 1 cup (250 mL) pear syrup. Sprinkle jelly powder over syrup and heat, stirring constantly, for about 2 minutes or until jelly powder is dissolved. Cool for about 25 minutes or until slightly thickened.

In a medium bowl, blend cream cheese and salad dressing. Mix in mashed pears. Fold in lime jelly, then the whipped cream.

Turn into mould that has been rinsed with cold water. Chill for at least 2 hours or until firm. Unmould to serve.
Makes about 10 servings.

This salad may also be served as a dessert, garnished with grapes, strawberries or mint leaves. For an edible Christmas wreath, make in a ring mould and garnish with red grapes or strawberries when the salad has been turned out onto a serving plate.

A birthday tradition...

Letting a child choose the menu for her or his birthday party is a nice tradition to follow. It is one of the many ways we can let children experience the satisfaction of making choices.

Comfort food cheers the hearts of others.

Jellied Strawberry Salad

"A delicious salad to accompany a chicken dish. I once served it with the Oven Baked Chicken Salad* for a bridal shower luncheon. It looked pretty and was a big hit. I since refer to that combination as my 'love knot' menu."

2	packages (85 g each) strawberry jelly powder	2
2 cups	boiling water	500 mL
2	packages (10 oz/300 g each) frozen unsweetened strawberries, not thawed	2
1	can (19 fl oz/540 mL) crushed pineapple, drained	1
2	bananas, diced	2
1 cup	sour cream	250 mL

Have ready an ungreased 8-inch (20 cm) square pan.

In a medium bowl, dissolve jelly powder in boiling water. Add frozen strawberries; stir until thawed. Stir in pineapple and diced bananas. Pour half of this mixture into pan and refrigerate only this portion for about 30 minutes or until set. Spread with the sour cream.

Pour remainder of fruit/gelatin mixture over sour cream. Chill for another hour or until set.
Makes 12 - 16 servings.

Use within a day.

* Found in the *Comfort Foods for Congenial Times* (violet) on page 20.

Preparing for a potluck...

When packing up food to take to a potluck, be sure to include any serving utensils needed. As well, if food needs to be cut up or arranged on a serving dish, do that at home. All of this reduces confusion in the kitchen, making it a more pleasant experience for everyone —particularly the hostess!

Lemon Coconut Squares

"This recipe reminds me of friendship. During a wonderful summer in England, a dear friend served these to me. Now whenever I have a cup of tea with milk, I remember the luxurious feeling of sitting in her garden sharing a pot of tea and some lemon coconut squares."

1 $^{1}/_{4}$ cups	all-purpose flour	300 mL
$^{1}/_{3}$ cup	icing sugar	75 mL
$^{1}/_{2}$ cup	butter or margarine, softened	125 mL
$^{2}/_{3}$ cup	granulated sugar	150 mL
$^{3}/_{4}$ cup	unsweetened fine coconut	175 mL
$^{1}/_{2}$ tsp.	baking powder	2 mL
1 tbsp.	grated lemon peel	15 mL
$^{1}/_{4}$ cup	lemon juice	50 mL

Preheat oven to 350°F (180°C). Have ready an ungreased 8-inch (20 cm) square pan.

In a medium bowl, combine flour and icing sugar. Mix in butter until mixture has the texture of fine crumbs. Press evenly into baking pan, moulding up the sides slightly. Bake for 10 minutes.

Meanwhile, in the same bowl combine granulated sugar, coconut and baking powder. Add lemon peel and juice, stirring until sugar is well-moistened. When base has cooked for the 10 minutes, use a fork to spread the topping evenly over it. Return to oven and bake for about 20 minutes more or until top is set and lightly browned. Cool and cut into squares.

Makes one 8-inch (20 cm) square pan.

This recipe can easily be doubled and baked in a 9 x 13-inch (22 x 34 cm) baking pan. Bake base for 15 minutes instead of 10. When topping is added, bake as directed above.

Comfort food cheers the hearts of others.

Marzipan Squares

"This colourful 'dainty' always made an appearance at bridal showers and christenings. Although it doesn't resemble traditional marzipan, it's very pretty and delicious."

1 cup	all-purpose flour	250 mL
1/2 tsp.	salt	2 mL
1 tbsp.	butter or margarine, softened	15 mL
1/3 cup	shortening, softened	75 mL
1 1/2 tbsp.	cold water	25 mL
1/3 cup	raspberry jam	75 mL
1/2 cup	butter or margarine, softened	125 mL
2	eggs	2
1 cup	icing sugar	250 mL
2/3 cup	rice flour*	150 mL
1 tsp.	almond extract	5 mL
	Icing	

Preheat oven to 350°F (180°C). Lightly grease a 9-inch (22 cm) square cake pan.

In a medium bowl, combine flour and salt. Using a fork or pastry blender, mix in the 1 tbsp. (15 mL) butter and the shortening until crumbly. Drizzle cold water over crumbs and toss lightly. Press into pan, and spread with jam.

In a medium bowl, thoroughly combine remaining 1/2 cup butter, eggs, icing sugar, rice flour and almond extract. Spread batter evenly over the jam. Bake for about 30 minutes or until golden brown on top. Cool completely, then spread with icing.
Makes about 2 dozen.

Icing

1/4 cup	butter or margarine, softened	50 mL
1 cup	icing sugar	250 mL
1/4 tsp.	almond extract	1 mL
1/2 tsp.	vanilla	2 mL
1 1/2 tsp.	milk or cream	7 mL
	green food colouring	

In a small bowl, beat together all ingredients except food colouring until smooth. Starting with one small drop, add enough food colouring to tint icing a pale green.

* The rice flour in this recipe gives this square its marzipan-like texture. If all-purpose flour is substituted, the result is entirely different.

*Comfort Food for **Sharing**, Caring, and Giving*

Sick And Visiting Soup

"At a time of family bereavement, my neighbour brought over a quantity of this soup with some buns. It was a meal in a bowl... and so good. Now whenever I want to take someone some comfort food, for whatever reason, this is what I make."

1 lb.	ground beef, chicken, or turkey	500 g
6 cups	water	1.5 L
1	can (28 fl oz/796 mL) tomatoes, mashed	1
¹/₂ cup	pot barley	125 mL
6	celery stalks and tops, sliced	6
5	medium carrots, grated	5
1	medium potato, diced	1
1	medium onion, chopped	1
1 tbsp.	seasoned salt	15 mL
1 tsp.	salt	5 mL
¹/₄ tsp.	pepper	1 mL

In large heavy pot or Dutch oven over medium heat, cook meat, stirring frequently, until no pink colour remains. Drain off fat. Stir in remaining ingredients. Turn heat to high and bring soup just to a boil. Reduce heat, cover pot, and simmer, stirring occasionally, for about an hour or until barley is tender. Taste soup and add more salt if necessary. Add a bit of water if a thinner soup is preferred.
Makes 10 - 12 servings.

Freezes well.

Foods that Say I Care

Food prepared with love nurtures and heals those who are ill or convalescing.

Comfort food cheers the hearts of others.

Broth With Tiny Little Dumplings

"This is a house speciality, especially during the winter cold and flu season. When I'm not feeling well, it makes me feel just wonderful."

4 cups	chicken, beef or vegetable broth*	1 L
1	carrot, thinly sliced	1
1	egg	1
¹/₂ cup	water or milk	125 mL
1 cup	all-purpose flour	250 mL
¹/₃ cup	minced fresh parsley	75 mL

In a large saucepan, combine broth, carrot and a small amount of pepper, if desired. Taste and add salt if necessary. Bring to a boil and cook for 5 minutes or until carrots are tender-crisp.

In a medium bowl, beat the egg, then beat in water or milk and flour to make a thin batter that can be pushed through the holes of a colander. Colander holes should be about ¹/₈-inch (3 mm) in size. If batter is too thick, add a bit more water or milk.

Place colander over the boiling broth. Pour batter into colander and press through with a rubber spatula or the back of a spoon. Immediately cover the saucepan and simmer for about 4 minutes. Add parsley and serve at once.

Makes about 4 servings.

*   Homemade, canned, or reconstituted bouillon base.

Garlic oil makes a soothing foot rub.

"*This old-fashioned remedy isn't something to eat, but it is made with food ingredients and definitely is comforting. Garlic has been used since ancient times for its restorative characteristics, and we find it is very useful when someone in the family has a cold or is just feeling 'under the weather'.*

"*The ingredients are **fresh garlic** and **vegetable oil**. To make it, place a couple tablespoons of vegetable oil in a small jar. Slice one or two cloves of garlic and add to oil. Cover and let stand for several hours, or overnight if possible.*

"*Massage the garlic oil into the feet until they feel warm and pampered. You can do this on your own feet, but if there's someone else to do it for you, it's even nicer! Put on clean socks, curl up in your bed, and sleep contentedly.*"

Broth with Tiny Little Dumplings

Comfort food cheers the hearts of others.

Lily's Soothing Chicken Broth

"For your good health, here's some Jewish Penicillin. I cannot tell you how much salt and pepper. As my mother used to say — as much as it takes."

4 - 5 lb.	chicken	2 kg
12 cups	cold water	3 L
1	onion, quartered	1
4	carrots, quartered	4
2	celery stalks with leaves, sliced	2
1	parsnip, sliced (optional)	1
2	dill sprigs (or 1 tsp/5 mL dried dill weed, tied in cheesecloth)	2

Clean the chicken well and put it in a large pot with the water. Bring to a boil and skim off the froth. Add vegetables and dill. Reduce heat, cover, and simmer for at least 3 hours.

Remove chicken and refrigerate for use in soups, salads, sandwiches and casseroles. Discard vegetables. Strain broth through a fine sieve. If possible, cool it overnight and skim off the fat, then add the salt and pepper to taste. *Makes about 10 cups.*

Chicken broth can be frozen in ice cube trays so small amounts are available when needed.

Chicken Noodle Soup: Add noodles to all or part of the broth. If noodles are uncooked, let them simmer in the broth until cooked. Add sparingly, as they absorb liquid as they cook.

Chicken Rice Soup: Add rice to all or part of the broth. If uncooked, let it simmer, covered, until rice is cooked. Uncooked rice absorbs a fair amount of liquid so use only a small amount of rice (1 - 2 tbsp/15 - 30 mL) for each cup (250 mL) of broth.

Hearty Chicken Soup: Add some of the cooked chicken, diced, along with vegetables of your choice. If vegetables are uncooked, add them first and simmer until almost done, then add chicken and heat through.

Chicken Soup with Matzo Balls: Cook matzo balls and serve one in each bowl with some of the broth.

Matzo Balls (Knaidlach)

4	eggs, separated	4
¹/₂ cup	vegetable oil	125 mL
¹/₂ tsp.	baking powder	2 mL
¹/₂ tsp.	salt	2 mL
1 cup	matzo meal*	250 mL

In a deep medium-sized bowl, beat egg whites until stiff but not dry.

In another bowl, beat yolks until lemon-coloured and frothy. Beat in oil, baking powder and salt. Beat in matzo meal. Fold or whisk beaten egg whites into this. Chill until thickened enough to shape into balls - about 1 hour in the refrigerator or 20 minutes in the freezer.

Bring a large, wide-mouthed pot of water to a boil; add 1 tbsp. (15 mL) salt. With moistened hands, gently but firmly form dough into 1 ¹/₂-inch (4 cm) balls and drop into the boiling water. Partially cover and boil slowly 40 minutes.

Remove with slotted spoon and transfer into pot of chicken broth.
Makes about 12 matzo balls.

Once cooked, matzo balls may be frozen on a cookie sheet and stored in plastic bags until ready to use.

*   Available in supermarkets.

A Change of Viewpoint

    Because I believe food conveys a caring message, I began in my adult life to take cookies or cake to friends who were going through bereavement or difficult times. When my father-in-law died suddenly, my own family received many wonderful sweets. There were so many that we couldn't use them all, and my freezer was soon stocked with these generous gifts.

    One person, however, brought us a ground beef and macaroni casserole. I can still remember how good it tasted and what a need it met at that particular time. That one simple casserole and what it meant remains vivid in my memory -- so much so that since then I have taken only casseroles, hearty soups or nourishing quick breads to those experiencing troubled times.

Comfort food cheers the hearts of others.

Homemade Butterscotch Pudding

"When I want something plain and simple to eat, this hits the spot."

¹/₂ cup	brown sugar	125 mL
3 tbsp.	cornstarch	45 mL
¹/₂ tsp.	salt	2 mL
³/₄ cup	water	175 mL
1 ¹/₄ cup	milk	300 mL
1	egg, beaten	1
¹/₄ cup	butter or margarine	50 mL
1 tsp.	vanilla	5 mL

In a medium saucepan, combine brown sugar, cornstarch and salt. Gradually stir in water and milk. Cook over medium heat, stirring slowly and constantly, until mixture thickens and boils. Boil and stir for 1 minute.

Remove from heat. Gradually stir about half the hot mixture into beaten egg, then blend back into hot mixture in saucepan. Cook 1 minute more, stirring constantly, then remove from heat. Stir in butter and vanilla. Pour into individual serving dishes. Serve warm or chilled.
Makes about 4 servings.

Keeping a "skin" from forming on top of milk puddings...

When milk is boiled, the protein coagulates on top of the pudding as it cools in contact with the air. To prevent this, sprinkle plain or toasted coconut on top of each dish, or cover with small pieces of plastic wrap placed directly on the pudding surface.

Comfort Food for Sharing, **Caring**, and Giving

Creamy Rice Pudding

"I enjoy this pudding when I'm not feeling well...and when I am! It's soft, satisfying, and not too sweet. I prefer it warm or at room temperature. In fact, if it's been refrigerated, I reheat it a little."

¹/₂ cup	uncooked long grain rice	125 mL
3 cups	milk	750 mL
¹/₄ tsp.	salt	1 mL
¹/₃ cup	granulated or brown sugar	75 mL
¹/₃ cup	raisins (optional)	75 mL
¹/₂ tsp.	cinnamon (optional)	2 mL
¹/₂ tsp.	vanilla	2 mL

In a heavy saucepan over medium heat, combine rice, milk and salt. Heat to a simmer, stirring a few times. Reduce heat to very lowest setting. Cover and cook for about 45 minutes or until rice is soft and much of the milk has been absorbed. Gently stir about halfway through the cooking time. When pudding is cooked, gently stir in sugar, raisins, salt, cinnamon and vanilla. *Makes 4 - 6 servings.*

Double Boiler Method: In top of double boiler, heat milk, rice and salt over direct heat on a medium setting until almost boiling, stirring occasionally. Place over gently boiling water. Cover and cook for 1 ¹/₄ - 1 ¹/₂ hours, stirring several times. Stir in sugar, raisins, cinnamon and vanilla.

The remarkable power of love...

We read an interesting comment in a nutrition textbook. A discussion about the controversy surrounding blood cholesterol concluded with the statement: "And don't forget the value of human love." It went on to tell about a study in which rabbits that were petted had lower blood cholesterol than rabbits which were not petted, even though both groups received identical diets. Thought-provoking!

Comfort food cheers the hearts of others.

Traditional Baked Custard

"My mother first made this for me when I was home recovering from the flu. In a pique of temper, I refused to eat something that looked 'slimy' but after she left the room I was so hungry I tried it, liked it, and asked for more! Since then it's been the food I want when I'm not feeling well."

3	large eggs (or 4 medium)	3
¹/₄ cup	granulated sugar	50 mL
¹/₄ tsp.	salt	1 mL
2 cups	milk, scalded* and slightly cooled	500 mL
¹/₂ tsp.	vanilla	2 mL
	ground nutmeg	

Preheat oven to 325°F (160°C). Have ready six 6 oz. (175 mL) custard cups or a 4-cup (1 L) casserole.

In a medium bowl, beat eggs until well combined but not frothy. Stir in sugar and salt. Slowly stir in milk; mix in vanilla. Pour through a sieve into custard cups or casserole; sprinkle with nutmeg. Set in a shallow pan; place on oven rack. Pour 1 inch (2.5 cm) hot water into pan. Bake for about 40 minutes or until set in the centre and a sharp knife inserted just off-centre comes out clean. Serve warm or chilled.

Makes 4 - 6 servings.

* To scald, heat milk over medium-low heat until bubbles just begin to form around the edges.

Acts of Kindness

Recently I came home from being diagnosed with a severe but relatively short-term illness. I stood in my kitchen, tired and discouraged, trying to remember what I had in my freezer to thaw out and have for dinner. At that moment, my neighbour arrived at our door with a kettle full of delicious, hearty chicken soup. This thoughtful action lifted my spirits and improved my outlook.

A couple of days later she arrived with tapioca pudding, perfect food for satisfying my finicky appetite at that moment. Then, a few days later, her husband brought over a large turkey breast and slid it into our oven.

These acts of kindness were not only a great help, they also said, "we care." I truly believe these caring actions aided my recovery.

Comfort Food for Sharing, **Caring**, and Giving

A Different Baked Custard

"Many people who normally don't like custard enjoy this one. The skim milk powder makes it creamier, and the brown sugar gives it a different flavour. It's a favourite in our house for both sick and healthy folks."

3 cups	milk	700 mL
1/3 cup	skim milk powder	75 mL
1/2 cup	brown sugar	125 mL
4	large eggs (or 5 medium)	4
1 tsp.	vanilla	5 mL

Preheat oven to 325°F (160°C). Have ready a 6-cup (1.5 L) baking dish.

In a large saucepan over medium heat, combine milk, milk powder and brown sugar. Heat to scalding.

In a medium bowl, beat eggs until well combined but not frothy. Gradually stir in scalded milk mixture, then vanilla.

Pour through a sieve into baking dish. Set dish in a pan; place on oven rack. Pour 1 inch (2.5 cm) hot water into the pan. Bake for about 45 minutes or until a sharp knife inserted just off-centre comes out clean. Remove dish from pan and set on rack. Serve warm or chilled.
Makes 4 - 6 servings.

Mocha Baked Custard: Add 2 tsp. (10 mL) each of cocoa and instant coffee crystals to milk powder. Stir to combine, then add to milk and brown sugar.

The power of care-full food preparation...

Food prepared with love nurtures and heals. Care-full preparation imparts a quality that is intangible, but nonetheless real.

Comfort food cheers the hearts of others.

Tapioca Pudding

"Tapioca pudding is a quintessential comfort food in my family — bland and milky. My husband, who is from Ireland, grew up with a similar pudding thickened with carrageenin, a type of sea weed."

1	egg	1
¹/₄ cup	granulated sugar	60 mL
3 tbsp.	quick cooking tapioca (use 2 tbsp/30mL if pudding to be served chilled rather than warm.)	45 mL
¹/₈ tsp.	salt	0.5 mL
2 ³/₄ cups	milk	650 mL
³/₄ tsp.	vanilla	4 mL
	raspberry jam (optional)	

In a large saucepan, beat egg, then stir in sugar, tapioca, salt and milk. Let stand 5 minutes to soften tapioca.

Cook over medium heat, stirring frequently, until mixture comes to a full boil. (Pudding will be thin; it thickens as it cools.)

Remove from heat. Mix in vanilla. Stir pudding after 10 minutes. Stir again 10 minutes later. At this point, the pudding is just right to serve warm. Garnish each serving with a small amount of jam, if desired.
Makes 4 - 6 servings.

Microwave method: In a large microwave-safe baking dish, combine ingredients as above. Let stand 5 minutes. Cook on high (100%) power for 5 minutes; stir. Cook on medium (50%) power for 6 - 8 minutes, or until mixture comes to a full boil. Remove from microwave; add vanilla and stir well.

Two versions of playdough...

When the children aren't well and can't go out to play, make some homemade playdough. Nothing is more fun than playing with it while it's still warm.

In a saucepan, combine 1 cup (250 mL) all-purpose flour, ¹/₂ cup (125 mL) salt, 1 cup (250 mL) water, 1 tbsp. (15 mL) vegetable oil, 2 tsp. (10 mL) cream of tartar, and a few drops of food colouring. Cook over low heat, stirring until thick and rubbery. Remove from heat, cool and knead until pliable. Store in a covered container.

For a version that doesn't require cooking, combine ³/₄ cup (175 mL) cornstarch with ¹/₄ cup (50 mL) warm water, then work in about 15 drops of food colouring. That's it!

*Comfort Food for Sharing, **Caring**, and Giving*

Jiggly Juice

"I like this recipe because it's made without artificial ingredients, something I think is important when people are convalescing. For kids, it's fun (and easy to handle) if it's poured into mugs instead of dishes."

2 ⅓ cups	fruit juice, divided	550 mL
1	7g packet unflavoured gelatin	1
2 tbsp.	liquid honey	25 mL

Pour 1 cup (250 mL) of the juice into a medium saucepan and sprinkle gelatin on top. Let stand 5 minutes. Bring just to a boil over medium heat, stirring frequently to dissolve gelatin. Remove from heat, add honey, and stir until dissolved. Mix in remaining juice. Pour into individual serving dishes or mugs and chill for 2 - 3 hours or until firm.
Makes 3 - 4 servings.

Fruit Jiggler: Stir in fruit chunks when mixture is partially set. Possible combinations are limited only by your taste and imagination.

Jelly Cubes: Reduce quantity of juice to 2 cups (500 mL). Pour mixture into a 9-inch (22 cm) square pan and chill. When set, cut into cubes and pile into serving dishes.

Make an eye bag for relaxing.

"I felt I was in heaven when a friend introduced me to the eye bag, and now I wouldn't want to be without it. When I lie quietly and place this over my eyes, the muscles are able to let go because the bag gently holds my eyes closed. What a luxurious feeling!

"To make an eye bag, select a scrap of smooth soft fabric that feels comfortable on your face. Cut out two pieces shaped as shown in the drawing. Stitch together, leaving an opening for filling, turn bag so seam is inside. Pour in ⅔ cup (150 mL) or less of flax seeds; the bag should be flexible enough to follow the contours of your face. Close the opening with hand-stitching, and that's it!"

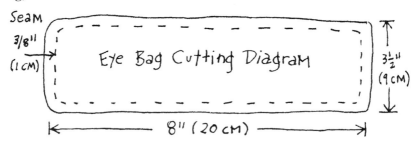

Eye Bag Cutting Diagram

Seam
3/8" (1 cm)
3½" (9 cm)
8" (20 cm)

Warm Soothing Beverages

"These are some of our favourite home remedies. Each serves a different purpose. When I'm feeling a little off kilter, ginger tea seems to bring my life back into balance. Hot lemon and honey is what my sons ask for first when they feel a sore throat coming on. And when I feel in need of gentle nourishment, a mug of rejuvenating milk seems just right!"

Ginger Tea

In a medium saucepan, bring 3 cups (750 mL) **water** to a boil. Add 1 ¹/₂ inches (4 cm) **fresh ginger root,** thinly sliced, and cover pot. Reduce heat and simmer for about 20 minutes. Strain out ginger pieces to serve. Stir in a bit of honey if desired.

Hot Lemon and Honey

Place 2 tsp. (10 mL) **lemon juice** in a cup. Add the same amount of liquid honey, then fill the cup with hot water. Taste and add more lemon and/or honey if needed.

Rejuvenating Milk

Soak 5 **whole unblanched almonds** in boiling water for half an hour. Remove almond skins. Heat 1 cup (250 mL) **milk** just to boiling. Pour hot milk into blender. Add almonds and ¹/₂ tsp. (2 mL) **ground cardamom**. Blend thoroughly.

Peppermint Tea

"*I read long ago in a book of herbal remedies that peppermint tea helps to settle the stomach. This is true for me, so I always keep some on hand. I used to buy peppermint teabags, but now I grow my own mint and dry some each summer to store for winter.*

"*When the plants are growing, I make the tea with fresh leaves. It has a different flavour from dried, and is very good.*"

*Comfort Food for Sharing, **Caring,** and Giving*

Honey Mustard Mayonnaise

"I like to give gifts of food that I enjoy myself, and this recipe is one of them. In our family it's a must with ham or bologna sandwiches."

1 ¹/₄ cups	mayonnaise	300 mL
¹/₄ cup	liquid honey	50 mL
¹/₄ cup	prepared or Dijon mustard	50 mL
1 tsp.	celery seed	5 mL
¹/₄ tsp.	dry mustard	1 mL
¹/₄ tsp.	curry powder	1 mL

In a medium bowl, combine mayonnaise, honey and mustard. A whisk blends the ingredients with ease.

In a small dish, mix together celery seed, dry mustard and curry powder until there are no lumps of mustard. Add to mayonnaise mixture, stirring or whisking to combine thoroughly. Spoon into small jars.
Makes about 1 ³/₄ cups (425 mL).

Store in the refrigerator.

Gifts of Food

Food thoughtfully made for others warms the hearts of both the giver and the receiver.

Jellied Honey

"For anyone who loves honey but not the dripping and dropping, this is the answer! It makes a nice gift too, as it's unusual and easy to use."

3 cups	liquid honey*	700 mL
3/4 cup	water	175 mL
3 tbsp.	fresh lemon juice	45 mL
1	pouch (85 g) liquid fruit pectin	1

Prepare jars as described below.

In large pot over medium heat, stir together honey, water and lemon juice. Bring to a boil until bubbles have formed over the entire surface. Immediately stir in the liquid fruit pectin.

Turn heat to high. Bring to a full rolling boil; maintain hard boil for exactly 1 minute. Remove from heat and let stand.

As soon as foam becomes a film, skim it off. Pour jelly into prepared jars, leaving 1/4-inch (6 mm) headspace. Cover with thin layer of paraffin wax (see below) if not to be kept refrigerated. Leave at room temperature for a few hours until set.
Makes about 4 cups (1 L).

* If you buy 2 lb. (1 kg) you'll have enough.

Preparing and sealing jars for jams and jellies...

To prepare jars: Visually examine glass jars for nicks, cracks, and sharp edges on sealing surfaces. Wash jars and lids in hot soapy water; rinse with warm water.

Sterilize jars by boiling in water for 15 minutes, leaving in the hot water until needed. Or heat in a 225 °F (110 °C) oven for 10 minutes. Keep warm until needed.

To seal jars: Cover hot jam or jelly with a 1/8-inch (3 mm) layer of paraffin wax. Melt wax in a clean tin can which has been bent to form a pouring spout. Set can in hot water to melt wax; keep melted wax warm until ready to pour. Pour the melted wax along the edge so that it runs in alongside the jar; this prevents air bubbles from forming. Tilt jar so wax adheres to the sides. Set aside without disturbing until cool.

If jams and jellies will be stored in the refrigerator, sealing is not necessary.

Comfort Food for Sharing, Caring, and Giving

Lemon Butter

"Lemon Butter is a great food gift — it can be used as a cake filling or for lemon tarts. Tarts are especially easy when made with frozen shells. They require baking before the filling is added, but there's no pastry preparation or rolling. Suggest them to your gift recipient, or give them along with the lemon butter."

3	eggs	3	
1 cup	granulated sugar	250	mL
$^1/_3$ cup	lemon juice	75	mL
2 tsp.	grated lemon peel	10	mL
$^1/_2$ cup	butter	125	mL

Beat eggs in top of a double boiler. Mix in sugar, lemon juice and peel. Add butter. Cook over simmering water, stirring frequently, for about 15 minutes or until thickened.
Makes about 1 $^1/_2$ cups (375 mL).

Store in a closed container in the refrigerator.

Direct Heat Method: In a heavy saucepan, combine ingredients as directed. Cook over medium-low heat, stirring frequently, for about 15 minutes or until thickened.

Microwave Method: Beat eggs in a 4 cup (1 L) microwave-safe bowl. Mix in sugar, lemon juice and peel. Add butter. Microwave on medium (50%) power for about 6 minutes or until thickened, stirring every 2 minutes.

Food made by someone else touches the heart.

    "I am particularly touched when someone gives me food of any kind. I always enjoy trying something new, and it's a treat to have a dish I didn't prepare myself.
    "But there's more to it than that – I am nurtured by the act itself."

Flavoured Butters

"I use these spreads to turn ordinary breads into special fare for a light evening snack. All are delicious with biscuits, muffins, scones, banana bread, date loaf, nut bread or raisin bread. I've also given them as food gifts — especially the raspberry and raisin-nut butters, because they're particularly attractive."

Orange Spread

$^1/_2$ cup	butter*, softened	125 mL
1 tbsp.	frozen concentrated orange juice, thawed	15 mL
1 tbsp.	icing sugar	15 mL

In a small bowl, thoroughly combine butter, orange juice and icing sugar. *Makes about $^1/_2$ cup (125 mL).*

Raspberry Spread

$^1/_2$ cup	butter*, softened	125 mL
4 tsp.	frozen concentrated raspberry juice, thawed	20 mL
1 tsp.	lemon juice	5 mL
2 tbsp.	icing sugar	25 mL

In a small bowl, thoroughly combine butter, raspberry juice, lemon juice and icing sugar. *Makes about $^1/_2$ cup (125 mL).*

Spicy Raisin-Nut Spread

$^1/_2$ cup	butter*, softened	125 mL
1 tbsp.	orange juice	15 mL
1 tbsp.	icing sugar	15 mL
1 tsp.	ground cinnamon	5 mL
$^1/_4$ cup	finely chopped walnuts	50 mL
$^1/_4$ cup	finely chopped golden raisins	50 mL

In a small bowl, thoroughly combine butter, juice, icing sugar, and cinnamon. Mix in walnuts and raisins. *Makes about 1 cup (225 mL).*

Citrus Spread

$^1/_2$ cup	butter or margarine, softened	125 mL
2 tsp.	grated lemon or orange rind	10 mL
1 tbsp.	icing sugar	15 mL

In a small bowl, thoroughly combine butter, grated rind and icing sugar. *Makes about $^1/_2$ cup (125 mL).*

*   It is essential to use butter, as it combines with the fruit juices; margarine does not.

Comfort Food for Sharing, Caring, and **Giving**

Peanuty Chocolate Fudge

"I was interested in cooking as a child, and on my eighth birthday I was given a Five Roses cookbook. I'd tried to make candy before, not too successfully, so I was delighted when I made this recipe and it worked beautifully. I'm a senior citizen now, and I've made this same fudge every Christmas for years. I couldn't begin to guess the number of pounds I've given away!"

2 cups	granulated sugar	500 mL
1	can (5 ½ fl oz/160 mL) evaporated milk	1
⅓ cup	cocoa*	75 mL
⅓ cup	butter or margarine*	75 mL
1 cup	smooth or crunchy peanut butter	250 mL
1 tsp.	vanilla	5 mL

Lightly butter a 9-inch (22 cm) square pan.

In a medium saucepan, combine sugar, evaporated milk, cocoa and butter. Bring to a boil over medium heat, stirring only until sugar has dissolved. Boil gently to the soft ball stage (see below).

Remove from heat; stir in peanut butter and vanilla. Stir until mixture thickens slightly (1 - 2 minutes) then pour immediately into prepared pan. Cut into squares when cold and firm.
Makes one 9-inch (22 cm) square pan.

*   Or use 2 squares unsweetened chocolate and 2 tbsp. (25 mL) butter instead of the amounts of cocoa and butter shown above.

Testing for the soft ball stage when making candy...

Mixture may be tested by dropping a small amount into a cup of very cold water. When the soft ball stage has been reached, it forms a soft ball which flattens on removal from the water. You will likely need to test more than once; use a fresh cup of very cold water each time.

If you have a candy thermometer, and live close to sea level, cook the mixture to 239°F (115°C). For every 1000 feet (300 m) of altitude above sea level, cook it to a temperature 2°F (1°C) lower than indicated here. For example, in Calgary, where altitude is around 3500 feet, cook mixture to 233°F (112°C).

Comfort food cheers the hearts of others.   41

Caramel Corn

"I make this every year around Christmas time and take it to my hairdresser, to parties, and to work. We also have it on Christmas Eve when the family comes over. It's so popular that I keep a 'just in case' batch tucked away in my freezer."

24 cups	popped corn	6 L
1 cup	butter or margarine	250 mL
2 cups	brown sugar	500 mL
1 tsp.	salt	5 mL
1/2 cup	corn syrup	125 mL
1/2 tsp.	baking soda	2 mL
1 tsp.	vanilla	5 mL
2 cups	pecan halves, whole almonds or peanuts (optional)	500 mL

Preheat oven to 250°F (120°C). Grease 1 or 2 large pans or rimmed baking sheets. Have popped corn ready in a very large bowl.

In a heavy saucepan over medium heat, melt butter. Stir in sugar, salt and corn syrup. Bring to a boil, stirring constantly. Boil gently for 5 minutes, stirring occasionally. Remove from heat.

Stir in baking soda and vanilla, then nuts. Pour over popcorn; mix quickly and thoroughly using two large spoons in the same motion as for tossing a salad.

Spread on prepared pans. Bake, stirring every 15 minutes, for one hour or until golden brown. Stir once more. Cool. Break apart any large clumps. Store in an airtight container.

Makes 24 cups (6 L).

An ageless truth...

"The heart of the giver makes the gift dear and precious."
Martin Luther 1483-1546

*Comfort Food for Sharing, Caring, and **Giving***

Index by Type of Food

Comfort food cheers the hearts of others.

Index by Type of Food...continued

Comfort Food for Sharing, Caring, and Giving

Index by Type of Food...continued

Alphabetical Index

Comfort food cheers the hearts of others.

Alphabetical Index...continued

Comfort Food for Sharing, Caring, and Giving

Comfort food cheers the hearts of others.

Those Who Helped

The authors created the concept of each book, set the parameters for content, and wove it all together, all the while writing, editing, and testing. They are:

Norma Bannerman & Laurana Rayne

The recipes were received in many different forms. They were written into a publishable format and typed onto the computer, thanks to the home economics and/or typing expertise of:

Karen Bayer, Jane Carlyle, Lynne Glatta, Pat Inglis, Terry Kopperud

Co-ordination of the recipe testing was kept running smoothly by:

Patti Rathwell

The recipes in these books were triple-tested. The first two sets of tests were conducted by home economists, who contributed their expertise to ensure the success of these recipes. The Alberta Home Economics Association, Calgary Branch, undertook this as a special project during International Year of the Family. Thanks to home economists:

**Lisa Anderson, Laurie Alisat, Norma Bannerman,
Diane Bates Christmas, Dora Blitt, Carol Blyth, Debra Brekke,
Marilyn Clark, Kathy Deyell, Faye Forbes Anderson, Fran Genereux,
Brenda Gracie, Pat Hansen, Sheila Heinrich, Joan Hickie,
Donna Horton, Glynis Joyce, Kathy Keeler, Sylvia Kong,
Mary McIntyre, Marie McNaughton, Susan McWilliams,
Shelley Mennis, Hilkka Mix, Lynne Moore, Nancy Nauss, Bev Peters,
Jill Pollock, Patti Rathwell, Laurana Rayne, Maureen Rice,
Helen Siemens, Kathy Simpson, Arlene Smith, Susan Somerville,
Sharon Speranza, Marian Spring, Donna Spronk, Louise Starling,
Nancy Vollrath, Cindy Von Hagen, Mary Wesley,
Carol Whiteside, Linda Whitworth**

The digital photography was created by pooling the talents of a food stylist, assistants and photographer. Thanks to:

**Linda Whitworth, PHEc   Chris Davis, Photographer
Linda Homenick, PHEc   newhaven media (Calgary)
Chantel Loubert, PHEc**

The heartwarming cover illustration was the creation of:

Richard Adie

The delightful illustrations inside the books were drawn by:

Brandie Cormier